THIERRY ROLLET

Edith Piaf. Ode to the child of a vagrant

First published by Editions Dedicaces in 2018

Copyright © Thierry Rollet, 2018

All rights reserved. No part of this publication may be reproduced, stored or transmitted in any form or by any means, electronic, mechanical, photocopying, recording, scanning, or otherwise without written permission from the publisher. It is illegal to copy this book, post it to a website, or distribute it by any other means without permission.

Thierry Rollet asserts the moral right to be identified as the author of this work.

First edition

ISBN: 978-1-77076-726-3

This book was professionally typeset on Reedsy. Find out more at reedsy.com

Contents

Foreword	iv
Preface	vi
Published works	viii
Youth of a Hugo or Zola novel	1
Edith and Religion	8
Edith and Men	12
Hymne à l'amour	20
The Success of Scandal	23
Fame	28
The Star	32
Non, je ne regrette rien	37
The Three Renaissances	41
Postface	45
Bibliography and Filmography	48
Biographical Summary	49
About the Author	56

Foreword

Was it not a challenge, writing a new work retracing the life of Édith Piaf, which has already been the source of countless books, films and images? But—to our greatest satisfaction—the challenge has been met.

Addressing Édith as a forever friend constitutes a beautiful entry into the narrative! This accentuates the topicality and intimacy of the author and his heroine.

Thierry Rollet seems to be in perfect harmony with because, since he was a child, her most famous songs—and, above all, "Non, je ne regrette rien"—made him resonate with joy, and he made his mother's devotion for Édith Piaf, and her talent, his own.

He wished, in this essay, *Ode to the Child of a Vagrant*, to illustrate—with an unpretentious yet delicate tribute—how the life of Édith, begun under the fatal auspices of vulnerability and misery, evolved in totally unexpected ways, just like a cataclysm.

Édith experienced moments of horror, miracles, happiness, love, painful grief—all of which Thierry Rollet reveals over the course of the pages, as if he had rubbed shoulders with the artist himself. Throughout this biographical essay, we can do nothing but be overwhelmed by the intensity of Édith Piaf's life.

The author has done a great deal of research to find the details that populate this beautiful biographical essay. In telling Édith's story, he reveals the feelings he experienced throughout this writing, up until the release of the film *La Vie en rose*, which is so moving and so trustworthy.

Therefore, let us delightfully imbue ourselves with emotions and memories, thanks to the talent of Thierry Rollet.

— Brigitte Willigens, *poet*

Preface

LETTER TO EDITH

Dear Édith,

I never knew you personally, of course, and I wasn't even a fan while you were alive. Indeed, when you had to leave this world—leaving French music like an orphan without a mother—I was 3 years old. And yet, it is quite true, quite sincere to tell you that your music has rocked my childhood, like a cradle would a baby. Indeed, my mother, who had a magnificent voice, loved singing *La vie en rose*, *Hymne à l'amour* and many other works from your immortal oeuvre to me. Besides, she is always very fond of recalling the moving memory of my third year on this earth, which unfortunately coincided with your definitive departure: as a small boy, stirring and awakening, I played in my park my muted radio, which did not stop me from recognizing and listening to one of last—but not least—songs: *Non, je ne regrette rien* (literally: "No, I regret nothing").

"Listen, Mom!" I said, then straightened out the whole of my small body. "Listen, listen! "Nothing at all!"

As a little music lover, I very eloquently revealed in that pleasurable sound while that "nothingness" resounded around me and in my head. Encouraging my good humour, my mother would increase the volume of the radio. In truth, that alone would have been enough make me wise!

Later, when I as a teenager, I admit that I let myself be more readily attracted by other music, of the kind that could hardly act as lullabies, including the rocks song of many English bands: *the Beatles, the Stray Cats* and *the Rubettes*, to name but a few. Had I forgotten you, Édith? Not entirely, even though the teenage years are an ungrateful ages in many ways. In truth, my sensitive and passionate airs—which emphasized all the fervor hidden within your small stature— reappeared in my memory only at the end of this troubled period.

Thus, in addition to the two titles mentioned above, I let myself become captivated by "Padam... Padam...," "La Goualante du pauvre Jean", *L'accordéoniste* and so many others. I also became familiar with the film *Royal Affairs in Versailles*, in which your character, the Woman of the People, sang *Ça ira* at the gate of the imposing castle. " "Go see it!" I exclaimed reverently, when addressing my relatives. "There's a Piaf at the gate!" But, I assure you, I was not mocking you; rather, I was using an affectionate phrase to refer to the worthy representative of the people of Paris, whom you embodied so well.

I have so much to tell you, dear Édith. I shall continue on later. For now, I would like to add a last note, which is the most moving in my eyes: when I went to admire your lookalike in the film *la Môme*, you finished this final, virtual show with the wonderful *Non, je ne regrette rien*. And in the hall, applause rang out, as spontaneous as it was frantic. I joined in this applause, cheered your last appearance onscreen. What better tribute could be given to that very same child who was so dear to the heart of the French?

Rest in peace, Édith. You will never be forgotten.

Letter published in issue no. 7 of the magazine *Au fil des pages*.

Published works

Novels :

1981 : *Kraken ou les Fils de l'Océan*, Children's book, EPI SA. Publishers, Le Nouveau Signe de Piste collection, 1981. Prize for Under-25s, 1981. (out of print)
2. 1992: *L'Or du Vénitien* (ACM ÉDITIONS)
3. 2001: *L'Impasse glacée* (Éditions du MASQUE D'OR)
4. 2004: *Le Fauve du Grand Cirque* (Éditions du MASQUE D'OR)
5. 2006: *La Voix de Kharah Khan* (Éditions Publibook)
6. 2007: *Le Seigneur des deux mers* (Éditions Mille Poètes)
7. 2008: *Je suis né sous l'horizon* (EDILIVRE editions) (out of print)
8. 2008: *Les Faiseurs d'Anges* (the book edition)
9. 2009: *Spartacus – la Chaîne brisé* (Éditions Calleva)
10. 2009: *Bushmen* (Éditions du Masque d'Or)
11. 2010: *The Prince of the Favelles* (Ex-Aequo editions)
12.

Anthologies of stories and novellas:

1. 1999: *Le Masque bleu et autres nouvelles dans la Venise du 16ème siècle*, Éditions du PETIT VÉHICULE.
2. 2002 *Vosgeaisons* (Éditions du MASQUE D'OR) (out of print)
3. 2007: *Contes et légendes des Vosges* (Éditions Publibook)
4. 2008: *Contes et légendes de la Puisaye* (Éditions du MASQUE D'OR)
5. 2009: *Cryptozoo* (Éditions du MASQUE D'OR)

Historical essay:

1. 1998: Jean-Roch Coignet, "Captain of Napoleon 1st" (Éditions SOL'AIR); reissued in 1999.

Biographical essays:

1. 2007: *Léo Ferré – Artiste de vie* (Éditions Mille Poètes); reissued in 2010 by Éditions Dedicaces

2. 2008: *Bruce Lee – la Voie du Poing qui intercepte,* in collaboration with Claude JOURDAN (Éditions Mille Poètes), reissued in 2009 by Éditions du MASQUE D'OR

Poetry anthologies:

1. 1983: *Au plaisir des rime,* self-published work, sold for the benefit of Noël des Autres, which supports unhappy children. (Out of print)

2. 1989: *Émois indicibles suivis de Pensées épurées* (éditions de l'ENCRIER) (out of print)

3. 2006: *Chants des Eaux and Voiles* (Éditions Mille Poètes)

Other publications:

1. 2000: *Scribodoc,* technical literary work (Éditions du MASQUE D'OR)

2. 2003: *Life in the Median in Le funambule and other short stories,* anthology
(Éditions La plume)

3. 2007: "Les Cent Chevaux ou le Rêve sans fin" in *Harry Dickson—Aventures inédites,* anthology (Éditions du Masque d'Or)

4. 2006: *Les Faux Amis des écrits vains,* essai (Éditions Mille Poètes)

5. 2007: "L'Anneau Draupnir" in *Harry Dickson – Nouvelles aventures inédites,* anthology (Éditions du Masque d'Or)

6. 2007: *Voir l'espace et mourir,* anthology (Editions du Masque d'Or)

7. 2007: "Pour le salut des Primanthropes" in *Voir l'espace et mourir,* anthology (Éditions du Masque d'Or)

8. 2007: "Un avatar malheureux" in *Harry Dickson chasse les fantômes,*

anthology (Éditions du Masque d'Or)

9. 2010: "Edvina ou le crime improbable" in *Harry Dickson face aux crimes impossibles,* anthology (Éditions du Masque d'Or)

Text published online:

Edvina ou le crime improbable, crime fiction, Éditions HIBOUQ, available at www.i-kiosque.fr.

Texts translated from English:

1. *Le Rivage noir,* a fantastic tale by Jonathan HARKER, edited by Jean-Pierre PLANQUE and the INFINI association, available at http://pagesperso-orange.fr/jplanque/Rivage_1.htm (original title: *The Shore In The Darkness*—unpublished)

2. *La petite Possédée,* a fantastic tale by Jonathan Harker, edited by
Jean-Pierre PLANQUE and the INFINI association, available at http://pagesperso-orange.fr/jplanque/La_petite.htm (original title: *The Little Possessed Girl*—unpublished)

3. *Balade dans la tourbière, a fantastic tale by Jonathan HARKER,* published by Jean-Pierre PLANQUE and the INFINI association, available at http://pagesperso-orange.fr/jplanque/Balade_1.htm (original title: *Walking Around The Peat-Bog*—unpublished)

4. *L'Adresse électronique,* novella by Audrey WILLIAMS, New Scribo Prize 2005, published in issue n° 3 of Au fil des pages (original title: *E-Mail*—unpublished)

One

Youth of a Hugo or Zola novel

A youth like yours, Édith, was never a youth at all: the period from your birth until you were twenty years old was but a sort of tunnel made up of mishaps, moving houses, physical and moral constraints…. It can be compared to a storm–a storm which–rather than having an instantaneous trigger, and whose duration was proportional to the fury of the elements–would have spread out over twenty long years, with flurries of unleashed elements, interspersed with false periods of appeasement.

Was it a warning of the destiny that would come for the second part of your short life? Maybe…. We'll see.

* * *

Not everyone can be a street child, in proper sense of the term. Today, would we see a homeless mother giving birth in the street? But in 1915, there was little talk of social services in the sense that the phrase has today. There was no question, then, of a household of "artists"–then branded with the infamous term *"saltimbanques"*, "street performers"–to ask for assistance in the event of an event that was as delicate as it was providential. Annetta-Giovanna Maillard and Louis-Alphonse Gassion would have to make do with their only child, on the sidewalk of the Rue de Belleville in Paris, facing number 72. In truth, resourcefulness would return to Annetta-Giovanna, alias Line Marsa, nougat saleswoman and street singer: she gave birth alone, without any help, because World War I took her husband and her only support: he was fighting the "Krauts," ("alboches")[1] as they were then called, while his wife struggled against suffering and adversity.

This fight would be recognized in the future: following the death of Édith Piaf, Maurice Chevalier had a plaque placed on this building:

"On the steps of this house was born, in the greatest destitution, on December 19th, 1915, Édith Piaf whose voice would later enchant the world."

This commemorative plaque is still there; the memory of the one who inspired it is still vivid.

It was not the time for artists and street children. In the face of the impossible, getting by was the only weapon. So, let's go on: street singer Line Marsa breastfed her daughter between songs, but her frequent trips forced her to alternately entrust little Édith to her grandmothers. The child's upbringing in a brothel house managed by "Maman Tine," her paternal grandmother, is part of the legend of Édith Piaf. Therefore, she was, from the cradle plunged into the cesspool, which the bourgeoisie scorned, without making the mistake of profiting from it. This "adolescent" century (it was only fifteen years old) had hardly changed since Maupassant's time–in the same way that his generous Boule de Suif was not allowed to be recognized by her travelling companions, Édith Piaf would have been no more if it hadn't been for the good fairies bending over her crib. That her bed was in between two brothel rooms did not prevent the child from growing in tenderness–the same tenderness passed onto her by Maman Tine and her (well-named) daughters of joy.

Indeed, who would have taken care of little Édith had she had not benefited from the affection and attention of so many "godmothers"? Surely not her mother, whose irresponsibility I will have the occasion to discuss further on. Édith would say this throughout her life: for her

---

[1] Hereafter abbreviated as "Boches."

mother, she had only rancor; for Maman Tine and her daughters of joy, only love; for his father, only recognition.

Her legend–popularized, first of all, by a book written by her young friend Simone Berteaut–would catch up with Édith again when her father, now back from the war, would return to look for her. "The real father is the one who loves his child," Pagnol says in *Fanny*. Louis Gassion loved his daughter, to the point of wanting all that is good for her: it was for her that he divorced the fickle and inconstant singer, that truly absent mother; it was for her that he would literally wrest her from the tenderness of Maman Tine, preoccupied as he was with making her a little girl "in the proper way". He, too, was the victim of bourgeois prejudice: no way would he let his daughter run about as she pleased in a brothel! Instead she would go with him on the road, where the Caroli circus passed, that gave the acrobat Louis Gassion what he undoubtedly called "his situation ". Him, he had a real job, he must have thought. But, far from being wrong, imagine for a moment what envious and ecstatic desires so many young children would have if they were offered the chance to join a traveling circus! Let us also dream…and understand that Édith's adolescence was tinted with dreams sparkling with rhinestones and spangles—a far cry from being sordid!

Of course, when we return to reality, we must admit that the dream does not fill a life, and does not bring home the bacon. Édith and her father had to deprive themselves simply to content themselves with the little they made, just as Molière and his illustrious theater had done on the roads of France. They needed to do so in particular when the circus abandoned them: what could two people do, alone, before a restricted audience, whose members were often more curious than generous? Once again, it is necessary to appeal to the magic, to the enchantment created by a small woman, 4.8. feet tall–this prodigy, this colossus of the lyrical arts. Did she not move the hearts of the passerby while singing, one memorable day, "La Marseillaise," when she was still a preteen? Would it be a legend to say that her career was decided in that moment? Perhaps... But here, the truth is incredible: Édith's nascent voice impressed her streetside audiences more than her mother's, even though they were singing the same fashionable musical standards of that period. It may be true that good blood can't lie, but then we would need to recognize that even bad blood can produce an artist. Even the worst land can help a seed become a big, beautiful tree!

Should we believe all this? Yes: it must no doubt be believed. It is certainly not Simone Berteaut's book–a "biography" of Édith Piaf that would become a best-seller after her death–that can accurately inform us about the various aspects of the truth and the legend. But the fans live more within stories, anecdotes, than truth.

Simone Berteaut and Annetta-Giovanna, aka Lisa Marsa, would still greatly contribute to shake up the life of the safe, rich people that Louis Gassion had nevertheless tried to stabilize hr–as much, that is, as an artist could. Annetta-Giovanna was left out of Édith's life when her parents divorced. Édith's half-brother and half-sister were born into of what today would be called "a blended family." But Édith's true family was the street. Louis wanted to preserve her family, but maternal atavism spoke louder. Édith's world was that of the Apaches, the Parisian gang. And Simone Berteaut, her close friend, was one of them: it was among them, and with her, that Édith would make her debut by adopting–both by taste and talent–her mother's trade.

At that time, the streets of the 1930s were probably less crowded, less noisy they are today. Even so, the era of the automobile had begun, and the peddlers and hawkers had trouble making themselves heard. The year 1932 saw the beginnings of the street singer Édith-Giovanna Gassion, who had not yet begun using her nom de plume. Édith sang; Simone, known as Momone, collected the money–a partnership that Édith would try to formalize by writing a "contract of engagement" for Momone, even though neither of the two friends was of age. Was this a respectable show? In truth, probably not: the future Piaf had never had the skills of a businesswoman. It was as time went on, over the course of months and seasons, that Édith's powerful voice was heard.

Some passersby stopped and set off again, some after having thrown alms. Sometimes, the coins would fall from the windows; Momone picked them up, collected them, counted them; she was trying to earn the 15 francs a day provided for in her "contract".

Meanwhile, Édith sang, trying to cover the noise of the street with the hot, intoxicating inflections that she was already capable of, and which would already begin to make her famous. It would take the intervention of one Louis Leplée–and his cabaret, *Le Gerny's*–to both create Édith Piaf, and to prevent her from definitively damaging her voice singing in the streets. Édith had her first gig! It was 1935; she was just 20 years old, and would already become famous! Having been noticed in the streets, she would now be performing onstage. It was another enchantment from the mysterious magic wand that had not ceased affecting her life: a prince charming, in the form of an impresario turned patron of cabaret, by chance remarked upon this almost dwarven young girl, endowed with a voice so promising that he hired her on the spot! What a beautiful beginning for this modern fairy tale! But this is what happened, and witnessed the transformation of a nameless street artist into a popular new attraction: carried by the same current as La Goulue, Mistinguett and others, like Yvette Guilbert, "the Sparrow" is born, followed by "Piaf the Kid," since Louis Leplée wasn't satisfied with the first pseudonym. After all, a sparrow is a "piaf" among the Parisian Apaches, and the audience of Le Gerny's wanted to get the best of it. Give a cheer for the Piaf!

The latter nevertheless had to comply with the iron fist of discipline: Louis Leplée was a tyrant who wanted to train a singer–a true singer, that is—and would not be satisfied with a product of the Parisian pavement. Édith was therefore asked to stop spending time with ruffians. They began by dismissing poor Momone, who they perceived as having had too few accomplishments, and was too much of an Apache. After many hidden tears–which she cried out in memory of her now-distant friend, whose tears she could no longer wipe–Édith finally gave up. On the other hand, Leplée could not get rid of the old Lisa Marsa right away, since her daughter Édith-Giovanna was still a minor; she was the first to see her daughter's talent. This time, it was with rage in her heart that Édith would literally take care of the woman who had never been a true mother to her, and who would henceforth live off of her daughter's income. But it wasn't until two years later that Louis Leplée was murdered, and songwriter Raymond Asso met with Édith, to break all contact with the Parisian milieu.[2] In the meantime, Édith began her career; she wasn't accused of the murder of Louis Leplée, and instead was saved by Asso from certain failure; artists don't easily recover from the consequences of such a scandal...

Some of the other consequences could nevertheless have preyed on Édith. Ceding to the very natural impulses of a young girl, Giving birth to a natural impulse as a young girl, she knew her first love in 1933. He was Louis Dupont, known as "P'tit Louis," also a pure product of the pavement–and he left her pregnant. It was only then that Édith discovered she was pregnant: the little Marcelle, whom she would bury shortly after the child died of meningitis. According to the legend, Édith, by then almost penniless, was able to face her daughter's funeral expenses? She barely made enough singing in the streets, and Louis Leplée was still far away. The only issue: prostitution. We need to ask that same question, once again: should we believe it? Édith, however, entrusted this part of her life to the journalist Jean Noli, whom she would meet during her last years:

"You know, (...) one night, after the death of my daughter Marcelle, I was missing ten francs to pay for her funeral. I had no money and I didn't know anyone who I could borrow from. So, you know what I did? (...) One man, walking behind me up the Rue de Belleville, solicited me like a prostitute. And I agreed. I went with him for ten francs. All to bury my child!"[3]

---

[2] For a detailed biography, see the biographical summary at the end of the volume.

[3] Jean Noli, *Édith*, pages 64-65.

Yes, no doubt, let us answer the question again: we need to believe this, since Édith herself believed it. But even Jean Noli didn't seem to attach much credibility to this sordid episode. He revealed Édith's lack of attachment to the children: "She tended to see them as noisy, smelly animals."[4] But that was also true when they were her own... Why would Édith Piaf have done less for her own child than Maupassant's *Boule de Suif*, which we've already mentioned in an earlier comparison? If the question is still left over, conviction–or even common sense, in the face of such a situation–can provide some answers.

---

[4] 4 *Op. Cit.*, p. 65

Two

Edith and Religion

Up to now, I've sought to evoke the series of "miracles" that helped Edith enter where we now call the "show biz"–what was then called, more modestly, or even more poetically, the world of singers. I should note that Édith firmly believed in miracles, even though she seemed far removed from religion, its dogmas and practices. Édith had always been a "free woman": had the pill and other contraceptive methods been common in her time, she would have recommended them without shame or walking on eggshells–or, at least, it doesn't seem like she would, considering the number of lovers who paraded throughout her whole life.[5] Long before Soeur Sourire became well-known,[6] she wanted to detach herself from morality and social conventions, braving them openly even in her relations with boxer Marcel Cerdan.[7] Nevertheless, she cultivated, in her mind, a

---

[5] See *infra*, chapter 3.

[6] Soeur Sourire ("Sister Smile"), aka Jeanine Deckers (1942-1974), was a singer and a Dominican nun. She enjoyed worldwide success with her first song, "Dominique," then retired from being a nun to continue her musical career. Though public opinion later renounced her and her music, " "Glory be to God for the Golden Pill" in particular, having cast the ire of the public against her. She died alone and riddled with debts, without having been able to renew her first success.

[7] See *infra*, Chapter 5.

strange attachment to the paranormal. Her faith in miracles was far beyond the religious and Catholic sense of the term.

It was, however, a nun–a holy woman–who intervened directly, during Édith's youngest years. In fact, after developing ulcerative keratitis, or inflammation of the cornea, Édith momentarily lost sight when she was only about ten years old. At the beginning of the 20th century, corneal transplantation, or keratoplasty, had not been developed, and little Édith-Giovanna would have remained blind had she not been the subject of miraculous intervention. The first protagonist was Maman Tine, her living grandmother, who–escorted by all her "daughters"–led the child to the town near Lisieux, in order to pray to Sainte-Thérèse. Maupassant, who portrayed the Maison Tellier in the eponymous short story, wrote that it was "closed for first communion." In this case, Maman Tine's house was undoubtedly "closed for pilgrimage"–another opportunity to show that the ways in which the Lord works are unfathomable, since He alone knows how to breathe His spirit among the women rejected en masse, and with horror, by a society of do-gooders. But what would she have thought of this society, if she had known the happy ending of this pious visit: that the little girl recovered her sight? What, then, is the purpose of virtue? No doubt to conceal the kind of perversity and malice that is often adorned with false colors.

Thereafter, Édith looked on Sainte-Therese of Lisieux, her benefactress, with a sense of solid piety. She even claimed to have seen her appear during the worst times of her life. Of course, these were times of ill-treated illnesses,[8] during which Édith even seemed to lose her capacity for reasoning. But, in truth, what is reason in the face of faith? Very often, a way to deny faith, which Édith, in her own way, never did. When being interviewed, during a convalescence in Saint-Jean-Cap-Ferrat, by a young journalist who asked her what counted for most in her life, a much weaker Édith replied, "Love! Is that not God's first

---

[8] See *infra*, Chapter 9.

commandment?"

The ode was, in any case, one of the greatest successes of Édith Piaf.[9]

* * *

However, for Édith Piaf his religious ties represented much the same as for the Latin American natives: from Peru to Bolivia, and through Argentina–where Édith made one of her last great journeys–the natives are devoutly Catholic, while preserving at the same time their polytheistic pantheon of gods and demons. According to them, the Catholic religion, its God, its saints and its blessings, are all means to fight the evil deities who could threaten them. Likewise, as I have already said, Édith Piaf considered her occult beliefs as being on the same level as Christian miracles.

Both helped her maintain her mental health during the worst periods of her life.

Thus, after the tragic death of Marcel Cerdan[10], the one who at that time was a great star of the lyrical arts would occasionally shut herself up in a world of fairground occultism —unless, that is, this was a more or less admitted way of defying morality and its conventions? Her relatives, in any case, did not see things that way. Édith's spirit suffered from the loss of a great love, even though their romance had been illicit. She needed to believe not only in the immortality of the soul, but also in mysterious invisible "presences," which can be called "souls," or "phantoms," if you will. The desperate lover needed hidden "contact" with her departed lover, probably to persuade herself, first of all, that she had not completely lost him, and then to find meaning, an explanation for those deaths that plunged her In a disarray that approached prostration. First of all, it was the unacceptable death of her daughter Marcelle, then followed by the sordid means which secured Marcelle a decent burial.[11] And then, years later, it was the

---

[9] See *infra*, Chapter 4.

[10] See *infra*, chapter 5.

[11] See *supra*, Chapter 1.

disappearance of Marcel Cerdan. Finally, it was "Guite"–that is to say, Marguerite Monnot, a pianist and songwriter who accompanied Édith Piaf throughout her career.[12] The terrible grief she suffered made her rely on crooks and swindlers, on the seers and table-turners that she summoned to her apartment on Paris' Boulevard Lannes.

Thus was the "religion" of Édith Piaf–a strange crucible in which she melted her despair in the hope of watching new hopes–new forces of life–emerge. Who hasn't been tempted like this? But Édith's fervor went decidedly further: given these disparate beliefs, we can see that her religion was composed of a cocktail of expectations, visions, deliriums, and perpetually boiling convictions, to the point of being an explosion. But is genius not born from these shapeless, even pernicious, mixtures? Édith was a genius, I am convinced, and I'll try to show this even better later on.

---

[12] See Decize (Nièvre), an elementary school named after Marguerite Monnot, who was born in this town (see *infra*, biographical summary).

Three

Édith and Men

*E*veryone already knows that Édith's songs are songs of love, like most songs, you would say. That is without question. But have we measured the role that love played in the life of Édith Piaf?

I will devote a special chapter to this theme.[13] I will first examine what role men played in the life of the woman who was a sort of anti-celebrity, but above all a woman torn apart.

There has always been a tendency to forget, during her lifetime, that Édith was not a sexual object, as so many men knew her. The narrow-minded ethics of that period tended to associate women with being reproducers, or even–if one had a more hypocritical, or simply more elastic, view of morality—to machines used only to create pleasure.

It is true, however, that the great social upheaval caused by the First World War benefited women because they replaced the drafted men in the fields and factories, which made them, for four years, masters of themselves, and even of their destiny. The boys' era dates back to the Roaring Twenties of the Interwar period, as well as that of the demands of female emancipation. The Communist newspaper *L'Humanité* went so far as to boldly anticipate it, with this headline on the front page one day : "Voting rights granted to women!" However, it was not until 1944

---

[13] See *infra*, Chapter 4.

that the provisional government of the French Republic, succeeding the French State, effectively granted women the right to vote. And Édith Piaf in all this? Was she a boy? A liberated woman? We must say it frankly: never.

When compared with men, Édith Piaf was, above all, a woman. When compared to society, she was an anti-celebrity. We will return to this point later.[14]

A woman, yes–but a liberated woman, no. Above all, Édith loved pleasing others. Her osteoarthritis did not prevent her from knitting sweaters that nobody ever wore, for she intended that to everyone wear them. Her thirst for human contact led her to submit to everything that was imposed upon her—except at the end of her life, that is. Édith could not say no, which is why many men took advantage of her.

Édith followed a path which we have already seen: she was an obedient little girl at Maman Tine's, and then, in the street performing tours she performed with her father. Gossips then claimed that it was from these two very similar environments–that of the prostitutes, then that of the street performers –that she drew these deplorable habits which led her, as it were, to prostitute herself for almost all her life. Nothing could be further from the truth. I'll say it again: Édith was a modern Boule de Suif; her character was that the heroine in a Maupassant story–the kind of person who gives her all, yet receives very little in return.

She made the most of herself as a singer, only to find herself very frustrated in her dealings with the men who launched her career, then with others whose careers she herself launched.

Louis Leplée is an exception, since he was, so to speak, a second father to Édith—but even so, he was a father who demanded results from his "discovery." Like Louis-Alphonse Gassion, who wanted his barely pubescent daughter to take part in his street shows, Louis Leplée demanded results of Piaf. Of course, he was far from disappointed:

---

[14] See *infra*, Chapter 7.

Édith, as we have seen, obeyed all the demands of this new craft, which she then discovered: that of cabaret singing, which would be her first stage that was not a street.

* * *

She had to play it this role of good student once again with Raymond Asso when, after the assassination of Louis Leplée–the question of who had killed him had never been answered–he experienced a period of lean earnings. After the cabaret Le Gerny's, she witnessed scene of the Vel 'd'Hiv' stadium, alongside Maurice Chevalier and Mistinguett, but the death of her first impresario left her without a protector. She had to find another. It was Raymond Asso, whom she had known at Le Gerny's and under whose wing she placed herself of her own free will—under the wing and under the body, that is!–who took on this role.

Indeed, the Piaf Kid started paying with her body in 1937. Doubtless she was not the only one; the world of spectacle had never been generous towards women. As for Édith, she was too grateful to Raymond Asso for complaining about the prison regime he imprisoned her with, and his demands for rehearsal. It therefore seemed natural to him that this collaboration–or, rather, this submission–should go on to include sexual activities. Also, Édith felt a boundless appreciation for Asso, who had, to an important degree, saved her livelihood. From the outset–when she called him in January 1937 to ask him to save her from oblivion–she submitted to him. It seemed natural to her that she should show him her gratitude mistress; her savior naturally became the new man in her life.

Édith accepted everything, forced herself to do everything, for Asso–whether that was the rehearsals, practicing for performing onstage, the working her already exceptional, yet still inexpressive voice: "She doesn't even understand the meaning of the sublime lyrics that she sings!" he once complained. It must be said that the impresario songwriter and coach was a former soldier, engaged at in the Spahis

18 years old, where he served in the East. From this former position he had developed habits of authority and predilection, and hence the discipline and songs he imposed on Édith: in her life, the Kid witnessed the disappearances of Momone the parasite, her Apache friends, and finally her father. In the latter case, Asso granted him a small pension in exchange for his discretion. Édith had to add languishing, if admittedly military-inspired, pieces to her repertoire, including the triumphant "Mon légionnaire"," which propelled her to the stage of the Théâtre ABC, where she was instantly revived.

* * *

Did men and success go hand in hand in Édith Piaf's life? No doubt, but not always in the same direction.

First, she would learn how to abandon her submissive instincts, because of the separation from the one who fashioned it, until she renounced the nickname of "Mother Piaf"; she was now "Édith Piaf" in the eyes of the public–a name she preferred, since she could thus recover part of her true identity. However, a new social, international upheaval was needed to "liberate" Édith: the Second World War and Asso's conscription in 1940. He disappeared from the life of his pupil, who was also his mistress. From that point on, Édith chose her lovers herself.

Raymond Asso's immediate successor was Paul Meurisse, a young cabaret singer, who would much later be known as a film actor. Meurisse, the son of a bourgeois family, became a singer. He contacted Édith himself, and then took her to his home. Édith would arrive, flanked by Simone Berteaut–who had always been "Momone"–but for whom the manners and Apache gait would not suit the distinguished Paul Meurisse. Instead, Meurisse put Momone to the door, so as to take care of Édith himself. Momone was furious, as attested by her comments to the media. When interviewed after Édith's death, she spoke of Meurisse with unconcealed contempt: "He unpacked his suitcase in front of us... Oh, dear! Laundry! Silk pajamas... And a collection of socks for three years in the future…and the toilet kit: it looked like a casserole!" Édith was not offended at all; on the contrary, it was Meurisse who would teach her good manners and how to act when among high-class society. She also had plans for him: they both met Jean Cocteau, who would write a play: *Le Bel indifférent*, in which they performed the principal roles.

Let's open a parenthesis: poet and playwright Jean Cocteau would always remain a faithful friend to Édith. It is he who, thanks to the aforementioned play, revealed Piaf's talent as an actress, which would then prove to the public that she is a full-fledged artist. By some strange turn of fate, they also died on the same day; the media baptized them "spouses in death". His relatives believe that Cocteau collapsed upon learning of the death of Édith. The poet once told the singer, "When you sing, it looks like you're baring your very soul for the last time." Thus, we can say that the Édith Piaf's "last time" would have to correspond to that of Jean Cocteau.

Later, Édith, who was enjoying her fame, launched many other young singers. The first was a group–the famous Compagnons de la chanson–with whom she would record an unforgettable success: "Les trois cloches." One cannot help but find, in their music, echoes of the war that had broken out: in the character of Jean-François Nicot, as well as in the knell of the Compagnons' voices, creating a rhythm for Édith's chanting…

During the Occupation, Édith would not return to the submissive relationship she had known with Asso, since she found a new impresario: Henri Contet. Exit Paul Meurisse, drafted during the war; she would not see him again! In truth, however, she also had two other songwriters, Michel Emer and Norbert Glanzberg, whose entry resulted not in new romantic trysts, but a new repertoire.

It was, therefore, above all because of gratitude that Édith attached herself to the men who helped her in her career. With each relationship, they did not share a mere friendship, but rather carnal affection. Did Édith develop friendships with men? Did she consider the possibility unthinkable, as do some narrow-minded people? No: you could not believe such from a woman such as Édith Piaf. Giving herself to those who help her was a natural instinct for her, even if morality suffered as a result: it was her way of life as an apparently liberated woman…even when she became the prisoner of a man!

Thus, it was because of gratitude that she was, for a very short time, the mistress of Eddie Constantine, when he translated the "La vie en rose" and "Hymne à l'amour"–the greatest successes of the small singer–into English. He did so when she was asked to perform in New York.

* * *

On the other hand, it was via her protection that she bestowed her favors on other young artists, whose success she secured. I will refer to those three which, to me, seem to be the most important: Yves Montand, Charles Aznavour and Théophanis Lamboukas.

Upon her release, Édith to a young singer who sourced his repertoire from the cowboy songs imported by their G.I liberators. "It's not enough," she said peremptorily. One needed good French songs. She thought American fashion would disappear from France with the Americans. Of course, she couldn't, foresee the success of rock and Elvis Presley, the King!

For now, a new repertoire, which fit well with the tastes of the French public, was needed for this charming beginner. And who would write it? Henri Contet, to begin with: at Édith's entreaties, he entrusted Yves Montand with a song destined initially for Maurice Chevalier: "Ma gosse." In short, Édith began to play a very complex emotional game: she would impose on her lover to provide songs for the new man in her life. Was not this a form of liberation, even if it was mingled with a desire to make herself happy and ensure herself a career? It's true that the former intention was directed towards Henri Contet, while the beneficiary of the second was Yves Montand. And what was to happen ended up happening: Henri Contet was eliminated from Édith

Piaf's love affair; since he was married, and not officially living with her, he would have to submit–that is, admit his eviction. This is how Édith Piaf launched the career of Yves Montand, while doing more for him than for Paul Meurisse, who did not owe his acting career to his former mistress. Yves Montand, meanwhile, made his film debut alongside Édith in Marcel Blistène's *Star Without Light*, then continued on his own in Marcel Carné's *Gates of the Night*–and finally, his career followed.

To some degree, Charles Aznavour took on the role of Édith's little brother. They met when he wrote the song "Jezebel" for her in 1951. He was never her lover: "It would be incest! Édith said when one dared ask her the question directly; it was the kind of question that did not offend her in the least. She hired him during an American tour as a handyman, taking advantage of his talents in that field, affectionately nicknaming him "the little asshole genius". You might say that Édith would shape the faithful Aznavour, since she even forced him to have his nose redone!

As for Théophanis Lamboukas, the young Greek man would embody Édith Piaf's final masterpiece. Who was he? A singer? An actor? An artist? None of these things: he was simply a hairdresser. But he was destined to become Édith's last lightning bolt, who would repeat, with him, the same kind of molding as Raymond Asso had done with her, as Pygmalion had done with Galatea.

Indeed, she would impose on him a craft that had never been his before : that of singing. She would even have to change his name, which the public would have trouble remembering, into a pseudonym that was more compatible with her feelings for him: Théo Sarapo, or Sagapo, a Greek word for "I love you". But Théo would be much more than a lover for Édith since she married him on October 9th, 1962. Their twenty-year age difference did not, it seemed, pose them any problems. Even so, many disagreements could have arisen between the members of this very disparate couple. In fact, Édith would impose on her new husband the same militarist regime she had known with

Raymond Asso. The unfortunate Théo was forced to repeat the lyrics of "À quoi ça sert l'amour" a hundred times–just as Édith had had to repeat those of "Mon légionnaire" under the baton of her new maestro.

But did Édith treat Théo like Asso treated her? That seems doubtful. Édith had trained several singers, whom we have mentioned earlier–Paul Meurisse, Yves Montand, and, no doubt, Jean-Louis Jaubert, the leader of the Compagnons de la Chanson–but had she done so in such a tyrannical and crude manner? "You're plugged up!" She exclaimed at every pronunciation error made by the young Greek man. "Is your head full of cauliflower? Are you a moron or an idiot?"[15] Thus the teacher's words were related by Jean Noli, who wrote of Théo bowing his head "under blasts of insults." Édith loved Théo, but in the manner of a tyrannous mother repeating her lessons to a tall, 27-year-old, whom she infantilized at her pleasure. Of course, this was more from perfectionism than wickedness; thus, the former pupil, who herself had become a mistress, would describe, to her last disciple, the complaints and demands she had undergone at the same age.

In 1952, Édith Piaf had already married the singer Jacques Pills. Their legitimate marriage had lasted only four years. Pills, meanwhile, had no need to be trained as a singer, since he was already in the trade. Is that why they never formed a real duet? Is that the reason they were separated? Yes, without a doubt. Édith could not treat him as she had with previous pupils. But on the other hand, with Théo, she found as favorable breeding ground as possible.

For his part, Théo Sarapo was Édith's ultimate supporter. Not only did he obey her without ever being rebellious, but he quietly settled the debts of the artist from his own pocket–without expecting to be paid back–during her final months, which she spent disconnected from the realities of the world, particularly in financial terms.

But that's another story.

---

[15] *Op.cit.*, Pp.118-119.

Four

Hymne à l'amour

"*L*ove! Always love!" Édith told an interviewer who had come to interview her at Saint-Jean-Cap-Ferrat. I've already demonstrated how she conceived of love in her mind: it was the essence of the life. It was also the main source for her songs–indeed, more than was the case for any other singer.

Beginning in 1947, the first date of her American tours, Édith Piaf became more than just a singer: she became a songwriter, writing herself the lyrics of some of her songs, after having been accepted as a SACEM "melodist".[16] These songs would become the most famous, the most adored by the public.

Here, I will recall one of the most beautiful of these songs: *Hymne à l'amour*.

We have always praised, and rightly admired, the intense emotions that Édith passed on to the audience via her music. However, her onstage attitude, her presentation, her costume did nothing to inspire passion: a small woman of some 4.8 feet, always dressed in the same little black dress, very simple gestures (with the exception of the song *La foule*), She always accompanied her last notes with a few, rather

---

[16] The Society of Authors, Composers and Publishers of Music, 225 avenue Charles de Gaulle 92528, NEUILLY SUR SEINE.

clumsy, dance steps. Physically speaking, there was nothing supremely passionate about Édith's appearance. You could not compare her appearance while singing to that of Marlene Dietrich when she was singing, nor to Greta Garbo, when she was performing comedic routines.

So, where did her passion come from? In her voice–this profound contralto, whose rising inflections seem to raise this tiny little queen of French song–Édith has always known how to create the fervor that animated her being. Her voice was the instrument of the exaltation that she brought to the stage. Édith Piaf had a voice above all, a voice that always seemed to come from someone other than herself, a voice that has always been able to express, in all its fullness, the feelings whose source lay in the depths of her being.

It was this voice, rather than the lyrics, that transformed *Hymne à l'amour* into what its writer and singer wanted it to be: a true ode–that is to say, a poem sung to honor a hero, a lyrical poem expressing noble or enthusiastic sentiments. This hero was Marcel Cerdan; I shall speak of him later.[17] This lyrical poem was the exaltation, created by the greatest love of Édith Piaf's whole existence.

Of course, some verses would do tend to make me smile:

I would go to the end of the world;
if you ask me,
I will dye my hair blond (trans)

Édith even writes of the laughable notion of "pulling the moon from the sky"! She surely foresaw this humor, since she added:

You can laugh at me;
if you ask me,
I'll do anything (trans)

---

[17] See *infra*, Chapter 5.

These simple lyrics, these unadorned words, seem to belong more to the diary of a 15-year-old girl than to the mind of a 32-year-old woman, which is how old Édith was when she wrote the song. But above all, the lyrics translate this true, personal expression of the feeling of love embodied by Édith Piaf. She would never stop recalling throughout her repertoire, even in her most "Apache" songs, like the "La Goualante du pauvre Jean," which repeats, as a leitmotiv, this edifying verse:

Without love, we are nothing at all...
We are nothing at all... (trans)

In a 1961 interview with *Cinq colonnes à la Une,* a TV magazine, Édith Piaf retraced the sentimental record of her life, using sublime terms to explain, when asked by the interviewer, what love had brought her: "But… Everything: the extraordinary, the marvelous, the ecstasy of life… I have never been disappointed. "

It was, however, the evening of the death of Marcel Cerdan that the refrain of "Hymne à l'amour," resounding in the auditorium in New York's Versailles, that the song would take on its true dimensions.

It is time to speak of the one who inspired her.

Five

The Success of Scandal

"Édith and Marcel!" Their love was so well-known that a movie was made about it… It is true that scandals always better attract the eyes and ears of the public. What was the situation, at the time of their meeting?

The era, in truth, was not tender with this kind of scandal: what would appear banal today was considered reprehensible at the end of the first half of the 20th century. This epoch, which was less decadent than ours, did not incite adultery in any way, especially when it was displayed in this shameless manner. The common link to our time resides in the media frenzy to which this adultery gave rise.

Let's begin by specifying who Marcel Cerdan—or rather Marcellin Cerdan—was. Born in Sidi-Bel-Abbes, Algeria, on July 22nd, 1916, he is a Pied-Noir. In addition, he was a born fighter: he started boxing at the age of 8, in Casablanca, where his family had settled. At 18, he fought his first professional fight in Meknes. On January 27th, 1943, he married Marinette Lopez. His career as a boxer is well underway, since at the same time he started in Paris at the Salle Wagram. His athleticism quickly made him a legend in the ring, where he is called the bomber of Casablanca. After winning French and European titles, he became the middleweight world champion by defeating Tony Zale on September 21st, 1948.

It was during that year that he met the singer Édith Piaf. He had certainly heard of her: Édith's reputation had become international, just like his own: she had arrived in New York, flanked by Les Compagnons de la chanson, whose success she absolutely wanted to ensure by associating them with an American tour that she already hoped would be successful. She is already hoping for triumph. Alas! It was a cruel disappointment that awaited him at the Playhouse Theater, where the Compagnons knew great success while Édith wasn't appreciated. The American public expected a little French woman as it imagined her, dressed in a suggestive manner, and not a simple little black dress. It was at the *Versailles*, in the same city, where success awaited him: his audience, no doubt more cultivated, and who no doubt attached more importance to that which had always made Édith famous–her voice–revered and applauded him. Édith was thus an American star who attracted prominent personalities: Eddie Constantine; Marlene Dietrich, who taught her English; Henry Fonda…and Marcel Cerdan: personal friend of the Jacques Pills and Lucienne Boyer, a couple of singers. This is how he was introduced to Édith Piaf, the small singer who had risen through the ranks of stardom.

Their love was a real bolt from the blue, undoubtedly Édith's greatest love. It's true, Marcel Cerdan was married, but Édith was never one to be meticulous about following social conventions. Moreover, her mysticism[18] led her to believe above all in a mysterious sign of destiny: "We were two French nationals in New York–two French nationals who were bored and friendless. It had to happen." For Édith, that was what solved everything.

Her sentimental life was complicated, in particular since she had begun an idyllic relationship with Jean-Louis Jaubert, leader of the Compagnons, and then again with Eddie Constantine. But Édith was like that, passing from man to man, to dispose of them as she

---

[18] See *infra*, Chapter 2.

pleased, and all for that intoxicating sensation of love. She delayed her departure from New York to watch Marcel fight the preparatory fight at the world championship. In Paris, the boxer would follow Édith in the small mansion she rented to hide their love. But even in those days, when the paparazzi did not speak about celebrities as they do today, it was impossible to combine fame and romantic trysts. And Édith and Marcel were indeed two celebrities, even though their worlds remain quite different. Thus, Mrs. Cerdan threatened to leave her husband when a newspaper scandal announced the secrets he was hiding. Cerdan abruptly leaves Piaf to rush over to his wife, who was threatening divorce. These marital problems did not bring him happiness, since he lost a fight in Belgium. Never one to show away from sensational titles and pompous articles, *France-dimanche* would estimate that "Piaf gave Cerdan bad luck! "

But not for long, of course. Back in New York, the two lovers knew success: Cerdan won the world championship against Tony Zane. From that moment, their idyll would become "*la vie en rose*," as Piaf dreamed–despite the scandal, despite the surveillance of Lucien Roupp, manager of the boxer, who treated his foal like a Spanish duenna. Indeed, it wasn't necessary for the failure of Belgium to be renewed, because a boxer can be beaten as much by the press as by a challenger!

Yet this is what happened in the end: Cerdan was beaten by Jake LaMotta in Detroit on June 16th, 1949. A rematch was scheduled for December 2nd, 1949 in Madison Square Garden, but it would never take place.

It is at this time that destiny would once again play a terrible truck on Édith and her lover. She became more involved with mysticism. Roupp himself felt troubled, since he would write Cerdan the truth: "*She [Édith] was burning with an inner fire. She lived every minute as if it were her last. It seemed as if she foresaw Marcel's premature ending, which she wanted to savor, every second of their lives.* "

Was Édith able to foresee the drama of October 27th, 1949? Cerdan had taken the Lockheed Constellation F-BAZN, on a trip from Paris to

New York, to meet with his mistress and train for his revenge against Jake La Motta. The plane crashed during the night of the 27th to the 28th, on Pico de Vara, a mountain on São Miguel Island, which is in the Azores archipelago. Out of the 48 passengers, none of them survived. Cerdan's body was identified thanks to his watch…which was a gift from Édith! His ashes were buried in Morocco, and then brought back, in 1995, to the Cimetière du Sud in Perpignan.

Édith was in a state of shock. How could she now reconcile her existence as a new star of the song in the United States with the grief that struck her so cruelly? It should be noted that Édith Piaf was now adored by the American public. Yet, as I have said, the memorable tones of *Hymne à l'amour* resounded, in a very particular way, at Versailles in New York, since the public was not the only one who witnessed its marvels.

At that point, Édith seemed to not want to live anymore—to neither desire success, nor to find any joy in living: the brutal disappearance of her lover plunged her into a profound nervous breakdown, which began with her being uneasy on stage following the singing of *Hymne à l'amour*, and then continued, during her return to France, by a deliberate will to reject being alive. Édith shut herself up at her home, lost her appetite, made several suicide attempts by overdosing on medication… Who could get her out of this depression? As faithful and persistent as ever, Momone–who had recently come back into the favor of her youthful friend–was determined to find a solution that would suit Édith's mysticism: table-turning.

"Édith had stopped eating," says Momone. "I had to find a way. So we started table-turning. I was the one who I interpreted the table's actions it: animated by Marcel's spirit, it would tell her to eat, and comforted her. That's how Édith was able to regain her balance."

Later, Édith would constantly repeat this esoteric way of recovering Marcel Cerdan's soul, until the last moments of her life. Since she could not do it without many other people, she would introduced her friends to mysticism, and all her relatives would have to submit, voluntarily or otherwise, to this fantasy which alone could reconcile her with her life and give her the motivation to pursue her musical career. The many table-turning sessions took place in all the places frequented and inhabited by Édith Piaf, notably in are s apartment on Paris' Boulevard Lannes.

Socially, Édith revived herself; she even seemed to put aside illegal love by marrying Jacques Pills. It was she who helped Marinette, widow of Marcel Cerdan, in the worst times that followed the tragic demise of the global boxing champion. The mistress, comforting the legitimate wife! Nowadays, this kind of spectacle wouldn't bat an eyelid, but, in the late 40s, one could witness this and decidedly say that one had seen everything!

Of course, it is difficult to control one's actions if one does not master one's own feelings. Personally, I think that the public did not want Édith to have displayed herself in this way with a married man: did this idyll, as ostentatious as it was scandalous, not give us "Hymne à l'amour"–which, even today, remains one of the greatest successes of this great little queen of French song?

Six

Fame

~~~~~

It's time to ask ourselves about what could have led to Édith's success. It's true, I've already written about her voice, but–other than its lyrical inflections–the voice of a singer is often and above all the bearer of its lyrics and melodies. Even rock music–and even the music of Elvis Presley, known as the King–could not dethrone Édith Piaf. American audiences remember her with fondness, and even those who did not know her would have in mind French expressions, which she had made fashionable in their country. Here I will recall one of my own memories: while talking with an American man, who was married to one of my wife's friend, I told him that I intended to write a book on the most famous French singer in the United States.

"The most famous French singer in the United States?"

He was astonished: "Who is it?"

" 'La vie en rose'!" I said.

"Ah! Édith Piaf!" he exclaimed. He had just given me proof that I was waiting: "La vie en rose'," an untranslatable expression in English, is now part of the common vocabulary in Uncle Sam's land—and undoubtedly in many others where she will sing, starting in the 1950s: Canada, Brazil, and Argentina in particular.

It was during these years that Édith won the Grand Prix du Disque with *Padam... padam*, and then celebrated a million albums sold, which was exceptional at the time. Her songs have never been referred to as easy songs–not even "La vie en rose," which she wrote herself, attracting the reproaches of Marguerite Monnot ("Guite"), this being the songwriter who she had since chosen twenty years ago: "You're not going to sing such a silly song!" What kind of inanity was "La vie en rose"? Well, maybe it was. As for me, despite my admiration for Édith Piaf, I never really considered this song, which always seemed very bland to me beside this *Hymne à l'amour,* that the supposedly righteous people of society probably considered it as being a hymn to adultery, or like other successes, including *Padam... Padam..., La Goualante du pauvre Jean, L'accordéoniste, Les amants d'un jour, Exodus, Les prisons du roy, Sous le ciel de Paris...* In that case, why has this "nonsense" been so successful? This raises the question of what is the popular song, especially the French ones, really are, and what appeals to it, in France and throughout the world.

Édith Piaf was the first to understand the reasons for this success: did she not Yves Montand to consolidate his nascent repertoire with "good French songs"?[19] The popular French song is joyous; it is enthralling, sentimental; and even when it is pathetic, like *Les trois cloches* and the *Les amants d'un jour,* it creates pleasure, because its themes are taken from the depths of the human soul. Édith had even known, especially in *Les amants d'un jour,* to add a touch of *mise en scène* to the lyrics to accentuate their pathetic nature: the sound of a glass that breaks, just after the final note. Thus, the loop is closed, since the song begins with "I wipe the coffee from the bottom of the mugs..." Besides emphasizing the inevitability of a double destiny–that of the lovers in question–the sound of broken glass accentuates the fall of the song, as at the end of a tale, or at the beginning of a new one.

This is what makes the popular song successful: its expressivity, rendered with a range of words that appear to be the simplest, but which contain so much emotion, by the frame and feelings, happy or

---

[19] See *supra*, chapter 3.

sad, revealed by the song as a whole. Thus, Soeur Sourire touched millions of listeners all over the world with her *Dominique nique nique,* or that Léo Ferré had one of his greatest successes when he expressed everything that could emerge from this apparently simplistic expression: "*With time, everything goes everything goes away…*"

Chansons à texte ("textual songs"), as they are called–i.e., those more intellectual, lyrical works–tend to elevate the soul. The popular song and its everyday words, in my opinion, elevate it just as much. To regard her simply as a singer of "musiquettes," and to ignore her, would be a serious mistake. Her letters of nobility are engraved in discrete movements–movements which she used give into the audience's sentimental balance. A love song–an eternal and essential theme–will find its way of into the hearts of people with all its weapons: the penetrating weapons of the poetic text, like the nonchalant ones of everyday words. Personally, I don't distinguish between Claude François' beautiful lyrics and melodies, and the profound expressions of Ferré, Brel, Brassens–who even defined themselves as popular singers! Claude François–to mention only him as an example, for they are innumerable–is by no means inferior to Ferré, Brel, Brassens, or Piaf.[20]

Fame, therefore, has nothing to do with intellectualism. Fame is constituted from the public's tastes, and the pleasure one enjoys in experiencing the work. A song that makes people happy, even if it has everyday words, is, for me, as respectable as the works of a great poet. It is not a fault of taste; it is simply a desire to live, to love life and the good things in life! I don't dislike those who consider themselves elevated by creating value-based classifications between popular singers and singers of *chansons à texte,* but I avoid making such classifications

---

[20] I devoted another book to Léo Ferré: *Léo Ferré - Artiste de vie* (same publisher). As I admire Édith Piaf, I have always admired Ferré. But this admiration has never compelled me to look at the favorites artists of my teen self: Claude François, Frédéric Francis, Dave, C. Jérôme…What did they think of Ferré and Piaf, I wonder? Probably a lot of good things!

myself: song is song, and it will continue to be the most humanistic work possible; such is its fate and its function.

An artist like Édith Piaf, who immediately chose her repertoire in music from the heart of France–even in its lowlands–must reconcile the tests of everyone. Her aficionados meet in all circles. The lovers of Baudelaire and Piaf will pour the same tears on the *La Mort des amants* and the *Les amants d'un jour*. Undoubtedly, even the pathos of Piaf will be found more moving: her laments, which have, as a background, the despair of humankind, affect, and will affect, all social classes and all cultural circles. This is the secret of Édith's fame.

Seven

The Star

There is no doubt that Édith was not aware of what the "star system" is; aside from the fact that the expression wasn't in fashion at the time, it wouldn't have meant anything for Édith, because she simply considered herself as attached to the lyrical arts. But her traits, her behavior, her mentality, her very actions had almost all the full spirit of a star in general.

It was in 1938 that the career of Édith Piaf truly began. Certainly, the discovery of Louis Leplée had brought her first successes, but his assassination called almost everything into question. One must remember, it took a certain Raymond Asso and his authoritarian training to create the singer.[21] But Édith Piaf, the star? She created herself, with good contributors, and, afterwards, good personal weapons.

In 1938, Édith Piaf was able to count on the devotion of the pianist Marguerite Monnot, who became her chosen and willing songwriter, because of the admiration the singer held for her, and then, later, on her connection of the actress Suzanne Flon, who became her secretary

---

[21] See *supra*, Chapter 3.

and one of her most faithful confidants. Successful tours followed in France, until the outbreak of the Second World War, and then in the world immediately after the war. Édith took meticulous care of it, especially with the performance of the show and the choice of songs she wanted to include.

First of all, it was her own, the first songs she wrote herself : *J'ai dansé avec l'amour, Où sont mes copains?, C'était un jour de fête*...Then she began imposing her choices for charming songwriters. As Raymond Asso moved further and further behind in her eyes, she received—or disappointed—many songwriters, some of whom were making their debut.

The first striking example was the young Michel Emer, whom she welcomed while he was in a soldier's uniform. It was in September 1940; the war had just broken out, and the songwriter had been drafted. Before he experienced this "funny war" that nobody expected, and to "spread his linen on the Siegfried line," the young man, passionate about music as he was, wanted to give a song to rising star Édith Piaf. She gave him five minutes, listened to *L'accordéoniste* for ten minutes before exclaiming, "I want it! "

It was thus, afterwards, in this way that Édith's choices were expressed: "I want it, I don't want it, I don't care, I'll look at it later!" Everyone, starting with the organizers of the tour or the show, had to bend to her desires, and even the caprices, of the singer. I would wager, however, that no one will ever regret it. If we take *L'accordéoniste* as an example, we know what enthusiasm, what conviction, what fervor even Édith knew to give in the creation of this song. The verb "to create" takes its full meaning here: Édith lived her songs like no one had done before her, transforming the last verse of the *L'accordéoniste* with all-consuming passion. How could one forget, like "the daughter of joy" in the song, that Édith "wanted to shout out the music" because of her joy?

She also brought the same passion to *Les amants de Paris*, the only song she accepted from Léo Ferré. It seems to me, however, that the song could not showcase his talents as well as could another song of the same kind: *Sous le ciel de Paris* by Jean Dréjac, which has an important place in French pop culture.

Finally, Édith's obstinacy in finding a lyricist for Norbert Glanzberg's music, which seemed to be the only one to impose its title to the song *Padam...padam*, must be mentioned. Many songwriters broke their talent on this melody, because no set of lyrics would please Édith Piaf. It was not until 1952 that Henri Contet's lyrics pleased the star. It was Édith's authoritative personality that ensured how very successful this song was. Getting such a result sometimes required more than mere obstinacy: it requires the gift of commanding, directing a career, and all that accompanies it, down to the smallest details of such-and-such composition. Thus the authority–and, at the same time, the genius of Édith Piaf–was exercised.

* * *

It was especially during the last years of her life that Édith became a real dictator. She could no longer bear solitude, so she kept with her a small courtyard of artists, songwriters, and admirers she herself chose daily in her apartment on Boulevard Lannes. Some famous names can be recognized here: Bruno Coquatrix, director of the Olympia; Charles Dumont, Francis Lai, Michel Vaucaire and Pierre Delanoë, songwriters; Claude Figus, a journalist, and finally her final male lover, who became her last husband: Théophanis Lamboukas, renamed Théo Sarapo and remodeled as only Édith Piaf knew how to remodel men, as I have already mentioned.[22]

Journalist Jean Noli himself was caught in the trap. Entering Édith Piaf's home was relatively easy; having its entrances required patience; but staying there quickly turned into a nightmare. Here is how.[23] Édith

---

[22] See *supra*, chapter 3.

[23] *Op.cit*, pp. 38-40.

Piaf's life was totally unregulated when compared to what everybody else would consider as a daily life. Having woken up around 2 PM, she was a kind of night bird, because of her various health problems–which were felt as early as the death of Marcel Cerdan, and aggravated in 1960–made her a martyr, which she ended up imposing on her court. Thus, all her pets had to be at her disposal at a time when normal people were in bed. Édith could very well call one of her songwriters in the wee hours of the morning to rehearse or revisit a particular song, whose music or lyrics were rather benign, but in reality she was trying to make a point. The rehearsals began at about two o'clock in the morning. Whether they willing or not, the songwriters followed the star in his lyrical demands. I personally award Charles Dumont with the title of most deserving songwriter: dismissed three times by the singer, he finally became one of her most assiduous collaborators, especially for the memorable song *Non, je ne regrette rien*. (I will revisit this later.)[24] He was, therefore, doubtlessly the one who was put to the test most often.

Moreover, Édith imposed her diet, and even her tastes in terms of shows, on her court.

Because of her deplorable health, the singer was forbidden from drinking even a drop of alcohol. Thus, table wine was prescribed. Her friends nevertheless formed a small "secret" reserve in the library; under various pretexts, they left the table in turn to go and have a drink. Not fooled in the least, Édith called them "bastards" when they came back; she herself was too supervised to be able to afford this kind of escapade.

She went to the theater or to the cinema as often as possible, but never alone: the whole court was invited to these outings, and sometimes even for shows with multiple rehearsals. Indeed, Édith was accustomed to see, and to see again, without tiring, a film or a piece that to appeared

---

[24] See *infra*, Chapter 8.

"fa-bu-lous," according to her favorite expression for quality. At each new edition, she noticed a certain detail, a dialogue that had escaped her, and which she watered her court with rave reviews, getting angry when she was not approved, or noting that such or such To him, nothing noticed. The small troupe was forced to see the film Pigeon de Monicelli eight times and to attend eleven performances of the Ionesco Chairs. And woe to those who complained or yawned with boredom: he was immediately punished with anger, with an obligation to see again the film or the play.

Having seen Édith's physical decline, the court did not revolt. The end of a star is always a kind of collapse, which one seeks to soften, failing to delay its inevitable end—which we shall see later.[25]

---

[25] 25 See *infra*, Chapter 9.

Eight

Non, je ne regrette rien

Starting in 1950, Édith's health began to undergo a significant decline. Her nervous state–which was aggravated by the depression resulting from the tragic disappearance of Marcel Cerdan–certainly accounted for much of this. Nevertheless, her main health problems stem from articular rheumatism, which at the time could only be dealt with via powerful drugs. Édith would abuse these drugs, and as a result she became addicted to morphine. Nevertheless, she felt the constant need to sing, from the stage, for her audience, to find meaning in life, and contribute to her psychological convalescence.

She did not abandon giving rehearsals or going on tours, despite the advice of her doctors. An artist like Édith Piaf could not be stopped, not even because of serious illness. No doubt she could even have sung, like Barbara addressed her audience: "My greatest love story is you …"

Édith does not lose sight of the concerts, the tours or the artists she helped whose careers she launched. Charles Aznavour was one of them at that time[26]: twenty-six when he evolved from "the little genius asshole" (Aznavour) and another affectionately known as "the big asshole": Georges Moustaki, whose song "Milord," set to music by the faithful Marguerite Monnot, would become one Piaf's greatest

---

[26] See *supra*, Chapter 3.

successes.

It did not seem like Moustaki, who was of Greek origin but who was born in Egypt, was poised to become a French songwriter or singer. It is true that he came to Paris to record his first, personal works in the 1960s, but that, following a strike, texts and music could not be found in the studio when he looked for them. Under the strains of time and necessity, he released a hastily recorded first album in Arabic, composed of popular Egyptian songs that he orchestrated with modern airs. He was smart enough to release this record—his first as a singer—under the pseudonym of Eddie Salem, which subsequently preserved his career as a francophone artist. His notoriety as a songwriter would probably not have sufficed to make him a household name, especially since performers, rather than songwriters, are more prone to this role.

Édith could not know anything about these particular beginnings, because they happened after her death. Her demise could have happened even earlier, in yet more dramatic circumstances, and by Moustaki's fault: he was driving a car, with Édith as the passenger, when he got into an accident. The accident delayed the tour, planned for the United States in 1958, for a year. It was during this concrete that Édith took Moustaki as an "American star," as she had previously done for the Compagnons. The year 1959 saw Édith repeatedly becoming uncomfortable onstage: "On stage, her voice dreadfully broke, her eyes blurred, she staggered, at the end of her rope. The curtain fell. (…) The diagnosis was invariable: hepatic coma."[27]

The coma was only due to her degraded physical state, but her relatives, as well as the public, believed her weakened by depression. This was why she would surprise everyone with the song that was to become her ultimate success, but which also surpassed everyone else in notoriety: "Non, je ne regrette rien".

First, let's examine the genesis of this song. Édith had confided to

---

[27] *Op. cit*, page 17.

her loved ones several times over that she needed a song that could give her a tonus, both physical and artistic, which she feared she no longer mastered. Indeed, she often stopped on stage, apologizing to the public for having forgotten the words of the song she was performing. This was particularly the case with *Padam...padam*, which itself was wildly successful. A 33-of-twelve track which I have often had the opportunity to listen to, recorded with an audience—Édith Piaf's last album, in fact—also contains the song "Mon vieux Lucien," which Édith sang twice, after having been mistaken a first time.

It was Charles Dumont, a new songwriter, who managed to give her what she expected. Having been thrown out three times, he returned to the charge with *Non, je ne regrette rien*, and then experienced the same enthusiasm, the same precipitous decision-making that Michel Emer had with the *L'accordéoniste* twenty years earlier. Indeed, even from the first verses, Édith exclaimed, "I want it!" She immediately told Charles Dumont that he had been able to translate her feelings, hopes and deep aspirations into song: Édith wanted to consider his past as "paid, swept, forgotten," and congratulated the songwriter on the choice of other shock formulas—"I don't care about the past," " I don't care," I'm going back to zero"—and especially with these verses:

With my memories,
I lit the fire;
My sorrows, my pleasures
I no longer need them. (trans)

Such was indeed Édith's deep desire: to create a kind of psychological shock for herself—a kind of mental cleansing— with a song like that. The public, which applauded her at every performance of this percussive piece, was not mistaken. You will recall that, as for myself, I paid special attention to this song while I was very young![28] That is to

---

[28] See *supra*, prologue.

say, behold the full impact that a work like this could bring to many minds!

A song of voluntarily returning to oneself; a song of renewed energy and courage, *Non, je ne regrette rien* was thus a deserved piece, and was going to be an integral part of the legend of Édith Piaf. Moreover, this song, especially in its last lines, announced Édith's happiness, reassuring the public:

For my life,
For my joys;
Today
It starts with you! (trans)

An involuntary announcement of her happiness would be found again with Théo Sarapo, who she would marry two years later!

Nine

The Three Renaissances

Because of her health problems, Édith needed to wait, without letting herself hope for a new renaissance, She knew of three during its final years, and even then, was not the only beneficiary.

She had hope, however: "Every time, when it seemed like everything was over, Piaf rose again. But could we really call this woman—slain, prostrate and soulless—alive? "[29]

Thus, she first came back to life in 1960. She wanted to make her return to the Olympia, despite her doctors' advice. Admittedly, her financial difficulties needed this re-entry: besides having no practical sense—spending, without ever properly counting—Édith was often the victim of friends, too interested in her successes by far, who shamelessly robbed her by making her pay for spiritualist sessions, which she believed would bring her closer to Marcel Cerdan, whom she had never forgotten: no doubt she was not a part of it, of the memories with which she had "lit the fire!" But, as I said in the previous chapter, it was indeed the song *Non, je ne regrette rien* that ended up saving her psychologically and physically, while at the same time saving Bruno Coquatrix and the Olympia from bankruptcy !

---

[29] *Op. cit.,* page 17.

An hour of music, with the new songs composed by Charles Dumont, Marguerite Monnot and Michel Rivgauche: it was all that Édith Piaf could afford, and, even so, with great difficulty, because her resistance was constantly weakening. At the beginning of the recital, the dismayed public saw her leaning on the piano, resting, for a moment, with her eyes closed, and then, a heartbeat later, call out to the pianist and conductor Robert Chauvigny: "It's fine, let's go! "

* * *

The second revival also took place at the Olympia, beginning on December 29th, 1961. This time, Édith appeared in fine form, as at the apogee of her career. She had with her only the name of Charles Dumont, who would become her favorite songwriter. He himself was entitled to the recognition of Bruno Coquatrix, who once gave him a magnificent costume and a choice of ties, all together in a box, on which the director of the Olympia had placed an engraving. *My dear Charles Dumont, you contributed to the resurrection of Olympia, and mine as well. Allow me to give you a sincere thank you. Sincerely, Bruno Coquatrix.*[30]

Charles Dumont would write Édith Piaf's last successes, then sing *Les amants* with her during a tour in April 1961; this was Édith's final tour. Marguerite Monnot perceived this preference toward Dumont as kind of a betrayal, even though she had never "let go" of her small friend. Did this disappointment precipitate the end of the friendship? Still, she died on October 12th, 1961, causing Édith shock and remorse that weakened her until the very end of her life.

* * *

One can be yet more elusive about the cause of Édith Piaf's third renaissance. In May 1961 she had to be hospitalized again; the doctors had spoken of cancer. But–in defiance of her sickness and of destiny

---

[30] Quoted by Jean Noli, *op. Cit.*, P. 33

itself–Piaf reappeared before the public scene without taking a break, even when everyone thought she was dying.

Of course, one can explain her marriage to Théo Sarapo as being a cause of the rebirth. But rather, was it not a new challenge to society, according to the habits of the former Édith-Giovanna Gassion, born in the streets and coming from the Apache circle? In the Puritan years of the 60s, the marriage–even of a celebrity–with a man of twenty years her senior, was enough to shock. Édith Piaf was 47 years old, but physically she seemed 60 at least. A passionate knitter of wool pieces that she never finished, she constituted her life with the same casualness, making her last husband sing a duet with her.[31] The shows–in particular, one at the Eiffel Tower, where Édith and Théo performed *À quoi ça sert l'amour*–would follow. Nevertheless, Édith was still in pain, unable to become stronger because she could not sing certain pieces that required a lot of breath and vocal power she no longer possessed; thus, *Hymne à l'amour* disappeared forever from her repertoire—but not from collective memory.

Édith Piaf's last concerts took place on the 30th and 31st of October 1963. "Then, slowly, she stepped forward, straight to the microphone."[32]

She received a full 16 minutes of standing ovations before she could begin singing, followed by, at the end of the show, endless encores. Certain pieces, such as *Hymne à l'amour*, were to be played only, since she could no longer sing them. Upset and overwhelmed, Édith could only lean on her microphone, murmuring "thank you" to the crowd. In such moments, her intimate friends forgot the tyranny she had so often made them undergo.

Her end was to be as fantastic, as original, as her work and life had been. She died at Cannes on October 10th, 1963 during her sleep, and was only declared dead the following day, when the carriage that had

---

[31] See *supra*, chapter 3.

[32] *Op. Cit.*, p. 49.

brought her to Boulevard Lannes arrived. Her young husband Théo wanted to remain faithful to the last wishes of Édith, who wished to die, or at least to be buried in the city which had seen her born. She is resting in the cemetery of Père Lachaise, in the same grave as her father, Louis Gassion, and her daughter Marcelle.

Her funeral was, of course, commensurate with her success: many personalities from the arts world attended. But did Édith deserve the disrespect of some people crossing the roadblocks, climbing the graves–picnicking in plain sight in the cemetery, so as to be sure of seeing her catafalque pass by? Édith had already been ruined by "friends" who had pillaged her house and bank accounts. She was never compensated. She was never refunded. But had she not already given them the best of herself?

No, not yet, since her memory, her frail silhouette–both bearers of a vocal power unlike any other–continue to make every generation shudder with a sense of the strange and fascinating. More than a memory, she is a kind of multi-faceted, multi-sonic giant, of an impalpable power, but who is never questioned, which still lives, and which always will.

Her statue, inaugurated in 1997, stands in the 19th arrondissement of Paris, Place Édith Piaf, not far from the street of Belleville, where she gave her first stammering performances....

Postface

THE TWO FILMS

Several films and documentaries are devoted to Édith Piaf and her life. And of those documentaries, to which I have been devoted, I will recall two that sense that they insist, sometimes in an innovative way, on the personality of the singer, and on the various themes related to this.

1- *Édith et Marcel*, directed by Claude Lelouch (1983), featuring Évelyne Bouix, Marcel Cerdan Junior, Jacques Villeret, Francis Huster and Jean Bouise:

This film is primarily focused on the meeting, then the passion, between the singer and the boxer Marcel Cerdan, who were both at the peak of their fame. In truth, the two years that this passion lasted are evoked in retrospect, since the film begins with the announcement, made to Piaf in October 1949, that Cerdan had died. To add to the whole, another love story is set in motion, this one between a fairly unintelligent prisoner of war played by Jacques Villeret and his wartime pen pal, who is from a family of nobles. Évelyne Bouix performed two characters: Édith Piaf, and Margot de Villedieu, because the latter is supposed to resemble strongly Piaf, who she refers in her letters to the prisoner. But she finally learns, during this prisoner's release, and from his first visit, that he deceived her by having her letters written by her lieutenant, who was played by Francis Huster. Thus, Margot rejected his prisoner, while Édith Piaf lamented the tragic disappearance of her lover.

For my part, I have very little respect for this film, whose two plot threads are joined by a link that is little more than artificial: the fact that Margot de Villedieu looks strangely like Édith Piaf. Évelyne Bouix seems to be much more useful in performing the role of this young girl, born of a good family, than that of Piaf. Indeed, what could be–especially in this context, that of an actress who is entangled in a badly written script and trite, "agreed-upon" dialogue–nothing if not a pale copy of Édith Piaf? It's true that the film does try to evoke pain and passion, especially when she mimics the song *Hymne à l'amour*.[33] But, once again, she cannot restore the authentic character of the song. Only the scenes with Cerdan appear truthful, especially because the son plays his father's role, and the script plays once more on the obvious resemblance between father and son. Yet, here again, everything seems to have been agreed to beforehand; it is not very inventive, and all the more so because this scandalous bond was performed by the son of its originator, which makes it all the more shocking.[34]

No, Édith Piaf definitely did not deserve this tripe.

2- *La vie en rose*, a film by Olivier Dahan (2007), featuring Marion Cotillard, Gérard Depardieu, Sylvie Testud, Jean-Paul Rouve and Catherine Allégret

Like the book you've just read, this film is structured according to a thematic plan. Via his brilliant use of the retrospective technique, Dahan shows Édith Piaf with her difficult childhood, the shocks to her system, her health problems, her career in various aspects–and, not to mention, her passion for Marcel Cerdan, or the singer's demise, which is especially dramatic.

Actress Marion Cotillard, it must be said, performs the part of Piaf with extraordinary skill. Her authentic performance does not lie only

---

[33] In this film, the songs of Édith Piaf were performed by Mama Béa Tékielski.

[34] It should be noted, however, that Patrick Dewaere was first called to play Cerdan, but his suicide prevented him from fulfilling this commitment.

in her clever make-up, which turns her into an almost perfect look-alike of the singer, but also by not being content to play Piaf, her passions and her character. Marion Cotillard *is* Piaf—as if she were coming inside her own skin, putting forth her performance with meticulous care, to the point where she can copy even the smallest gestures of her model. So, it's not surprising that she received the Oscar for Best Actress. The film itself won two Oscars, three Césars, two Czech Lions, and a Golden Globe–outstanding awards for a French film.

I went to see it in theaters, and I still want to remember that, at the end, when the last image faded on a performance of "Non, je ne regrette rien," a huge moment of emotion seized this small, provincial theater. I have already referred to the crackling applause that accompanied it,[35] which were like a last collective salvation, as if the ghost of Édith Piaf had suddenly haunted the room, making me believe in the resurrection of this small, great lady…

I think my desire to write this book dates from that time.

---

[35] See *supra*, Prologue.

Bibliography and Filmography

I have quoted several of my sources many times in this book. I will review the main ones for clarity:

- *Édith*, book by Jean Noli, Éditions Stock, 1973
- *Édith Piaf*, book by Stan Cuesta, Editions EJL, coll. Librio, 2000
- *Édith Piaf : Une brève rencontre*, documentary by Michel Wyn, 1994
- *Édith Piaf*, collector's edition, ARTE 2 DVD:
  o *Sans amour on est rien du tout* (DVD 1)
  o *Le Best Of des concerts* (DVD 2)
- *Les derniers jours d'Édith Piaf*, film by Michel Pichon (2008)

* * *

In addition to the popular encyclopedia Wikipedia and the websites of the films, Édith Piaf's estate maintains an official website: http://piafedith.free.fr.

Biographical Summary

Édith Piaf (1915-1963)

- **1915:** birth of Édith-Giovanna Gassion in front of 72 Rue de Belleville (Paris, 19th arrondissement). In 1966, on the building located at this address, a plaque was inaugurated by Maurice Chevalier: *"Born, on the steps of this house, on December 19th, 1915, in the greatest destitution, Édith Piaf, whose voice would later to enchant the world."* Her mother, Annetta-Giovanna Maillard, born of a French father and a Kabyle mother, sells nougat in the street and sings under the pseudonym of Line Marsa. Her father, Louis-Alphonse Gassion, is a circus contortionist. The parents married in 1914, when the First World War broke out and the father was drafted for war.
- **1915-1925:** With her father away at war, and her "lyric artist" mother choosing not to care for her, Édith is raised alternately by her two grandmothers: first her maternal grandmother, Aïcha Maillard, then by her paternal grandmother, Louise-Léontine Gassion, known as "Maman Tine"…who ran a prostitution house in Bernay (Eure).
- **1925-1930:** Édith becomes an entertainer for the company of her father who, now back from the war, works as an artist at the circus Caroli. Then, the father and the daughter are alone in town squares, traveling from city to city: Louis is doing the tours de force, while Édith collects the money. One day, the little girl drew her first success singing the *Marseillaise* in the street, before the spectators who, touched by her song, were more generous than usual. From then on, the itinerant show

would always with a song by Édith, who performed the fashionable songs of the day: *Nuits de Chine, Voici mon coeur...*

- **1929:** Louis Gassion divorces his wife for being too fickle, then remarries, thereby giving Édith a half-sister: Denise. Édith already has a brother, Herbert—or, rather, a half-brother, since Louis had denied being the father. The first meeting of Édith and her future best friend, Simone Berteaut, known as Momone, who would one day write a best-seller about the life of Édith Piaf.
- **1932:** Édith sings in the courtyards of the building while Momone collects the money. Édith even "officially" hired Momone as an impresario, "for a salary of 15 francs a day." In truth, it is her mother who would receive the money, Édith being a minor–which doesn't prevent her from living very freely, here and there, frequenting "Apache" gangs, without her parents exercising genuine surveillance over her.
- **1933:** Édith begins first great love with Louis Dupont, known as P'tit Louis. Pregnant, she gives birth to her only child: Marcelle, nicknamed "Cecelle," who soon dies from meningitis.
- **1935:** Louis Leplée, a former artist turned impresario, notices Édith as she sings in the street and invites her to sing in his cabaret, Gerny's, located at 54 rue Pierre Charron. She sings *Nini peau d'chien* and Vincent Scotto's *Les Mômes de la Cloche* before a prestigious clientèle: Marcel Bleustein-Blanchet, Joseph Kessel, Jean Mermoz, Maurice Chevalier… Leplée develops Édith's first pseudonym: the Piaf Kid, in reference to her small size: 4.8 feet. On October 26th, Édith sings on *Radio-Cité*, a show by Leplée's friend Jacques Canetti. Her career was launched thanks to them.
- **December 18th, 1935:** the date when Édith recorded her first album with Polydor, a brand owned by Canetti. There she meets Robert Juel, who will become her *L'accordéoniste* and Marguerite Monnot, her future songwriter. Born in 1903 in Decize (Nièvre), Marguerite Monnot is a pianist who already holds several awards, including one for having performed Chopin.

- **1936:** The Piaf Kid begins a prestigious career; her poster even shared space at the Vél 'd'Hiv' stadium with Maurice Chevalier, Mistinguett, Fernandel and Albert Préjean. It even began with La Garçonne, a film by Jean de Limur, in which she sings music written by Jean Wiener. On April 6th, she goes to the home of "Papa Leplée," where she is greeted by the police and placed in police custody: Leplée had just been assassinated. How much the Piaf Mother's reputation would suffer from the repercussions of this crime is never determined: for a whole, she would only song in cabarets. She, will, however return on stage with a new impresario, Fernand Lumbroso, the future director of Théâtre Mogador. It is nevertheless a period of meager earnings...
- **1937:** Mother Piaf" rows her boat" as long as she can. Having launched a genuine appeal to help the songwriter Raymond Asso, whom she had known at Gerny's, she will experience an artistic renaissance, with a piece that will become a hit for the time: *Mon légionnaire*. Asso will shape Édith Piaf; her pseudonym became official, with great care. On his instructions, she breaks her friendship with Momone; with her Apache friends; and with her father, to whom Asso pays a small compensatory pension... Having become her lover, Asso taught Édith everything: stage, maintenance, lifestyle, voice work...and he writes new songs, recorded at the Polydor: *Le Fanion de la Légion, Paris-Méditerranée, Browning, Je n'en connais pas la fin*.
- **1938:** a year of concerts and triumphant tours for Édith Piaf, who has become an authentic star. Future comedian Suzanne Flon becomes her secretary, and Marguerite Monnot, her official songwriting partner.
- **1939:** Édith Piaf builds her career, learning to do without Asso, whom she was beginning to love less, little by little. The war will definitely separate them: Asso is drafted. Édith will forget him in the arms of a young cabaret singer, Paul Meurisse, with whom she will start a new relationship. It is at this time that she begins to write songs herself, set to music by Marguerite Monnot: *J'ai dansé avec l'amour, Où sont-ils mes petits copains, C'était un jour de fête...*

- **1940:** Édith Piaf's career undergoes a new turning point: it now she who chooses her lyricists and songwriters. A young soldier, Michel Emer, proposes the *L'accordéoniste* to her, which she immediately accepts, after having nearly rejected it. She then begins a faithful friendship with the poet Jean Cocteau, who wrote a one-act play, *Le Bel Indifférent*, for her . Édith becomes an actress, as well as Paul Meurisse, for whom she is soliciting a role...and a reprieve of 6 days, at the time of his drafting.
- **1941-1944:** Despite the French occupation, Édith continues her career, her concerts, her tours. In 1943 and 1944, she goes to Germany to sing for French prisoners. Louis Gassion dies in March 1944. At the Liberation of Paris, Édith Piaf will be questioned because she sang for the enemy, but will be approved by proving that she has allowed friends to hide or escape: Michel Emer, Norbert Glanzberg and Henri Contet, who composed a new repertoire, which was very different from Asso's. Starting at that time, Henri Contet will replace Paul Meurisse as Édith's lover.
- **1945:** Édith Piaf takes in a new foal, a creative young singer by the name of Yves Montand, whom she met the previous year during a show at the Moulin Rouge. She finds him "good French songs," some signed by Loulou Gasté and Henri Contet, who will be replaced as Édith's lover. She will write music for him herself. This is the beginning of a long collaboration. Yves Montand will also make his first steps as a film actor in *Star Without Light*, a film by Marcel Blistène, in which Édith is the star. In the same year, Montand receives his first major role in Marcel Carné's *Gates of the Night*. This pivotal year of Piaf's career also saw the creation of the international success *La Vie en rose*, for Marcel Louiguy will sign on the music.
- **1946:** Édith goes on tour with 8 beginning singers—a new discovery, a new launch: the Compagnons de la Chanson, with whom she will write the song *Les Trois Cloches*, which will be very successful at Le Club des cinq. She leaves Yves Montand for Jean-Louis Jaubert, "leader" of the Compagnons, and Polydor Records or Pathé-Marconi

(now EMI). On May 16th, she gives a large concert, with an orchestra of 60 musicians, at the Palais de Chaillot.

- **1947-1948:** Louis Barrier, one of Piaf's impresarios, signed a contract with the Playhouse Theater in New York. *Piaf,* on Broadway, is the event of the year. Half-failure: the public prefers the Compagnons. At the Versailles in the same city, on the other hand, it enjoys 8 weeks of uninterrupted success. During this visit, Édith met people who would shape her existence, among them actress Marlene Dietrich, and the couple Jacques Pills and Lucienne Boyer, who would introduce the boxer Marcel Cerdan, one of the great passions in her life. Their liaison caused a scandal, since Cerdan is married. Édith makes no secret of it; she asked Cerdan to join her onstage at one of her American concerts; she will return to the US several times. The fury of the media is unleashed, depending on whether or not "the bomber of Casablanca" wins or loses his fights.
- **1949:** Cerdan loses his life in a plane crash bringing him to the US, to fight a fight against Jake LaMotta...and to join Piaf. Desperate, Édith sings for him at Versailles that same evening, and faints onstage after performing *Hymne à l'amour.*
- **1950:** Life for Piaf begins to get painful: articular rheumatism will cause her to become addicted to morphine, and will force her to look for detoxifying cures. However, she does concerts in the US, writing *Hymn To Love*, an American version of *Hymne à l'amour*, for which Eddie Constantine composed the lyrics (he was to become Édith's new lover). She will launch the career of a new French singer and songwriter: Charles Aznavour.
- **1951:** Édith is the star of the musical *La P'tite Lili* (libretto by Marcel Achard, music by Marguerite Monnot). She recorded songs written by Aznavour: *Plus bleu que tes yeux, Jézabel, Je hais les dimanches.*
- **1952:** Édith receives the Grand Prix du Disque with the song *Padam... Padam...* (lyrics by Henri Contet, music by Norbert Glanzberg). On July 29, she marries singer Jacques Pills, with whom she does not form a genuine duo—they sing in separate rooms or separately on the

same stage–and they will still go on tour to the US.
- **1953:** release of the film *Royal Affairs in Versailles*, directed by Sacha Guitry, in which Édith sings "Ça ira".
- **1954-1955:** Édith Piaf celebrates one million records sold, which at the time is exceptional. Creation of the *La Goualante du pauvre Jean* and discovery of new songwriters: Jean Dréjac (_Sous le ciel de Paris_) and Michel Rivgauche (_Les prisons du roy_, *Salle d'attente*).
- **1956:** Édith Piaf and Jacques Pills divorce. World tour: US, Quebec, Rio de Janeiro, Buenos Aires.
- **1957:** Recording of *La foule*, which was an adaptation, by Michel Rivgauche, of a melody by Angel Cabral, which Édith had brought back from Argentina. Shooting of Blistène's *Les Amants de demain*.
- **1958:** Show at the Olympia from February to May. Édith Piaf will launch a new beginner, Félix Marten—and make him his new lover. She hires Charles Dumont, but agrees on another young beginner: Georges Moustaki, known as Jo. She will take the "American star" with her to a new tour of the US. But they will have a serious car accident (Moustaki was driving) that pushes the tour to the following year.
- **1959:** American tour. Creation of *Milord* (lyrics by Moustaki, music by Marguerite Monnot). Having undergone attacks onstage, Édith is hospitalized twice, and is undergoing a serious financial crisis. A further car accident in June breaks her ribs. Édith Piaf tries to continue on, to continue performances and tours, despite the advice of her doctor and despite relapses and feelings of unease, which come one after the other.
- **1960:** Édith Piaf goes repeatedly to the hospital, which requires her to bring her show back to the Olympia. The newspaper emphasized the whole affair: she is said to be ruined, dying... It is revealed that Bruno Coquatrix counts on her future successes to prevent the Olympia, which is on the verge of bankruptcy, from closing down. In October, Charles Dumont returns to the charge: he is finally accepted with his song *Non, je ne regrette rien*. Édith Piaf will record 12 pieces of his before the end of the year, including *Mon Dieu, Mon vieux Lucien* and

Les Flonflons du bal.

- **1961:** Édith Piaf has been at the Olympia since December 29th, 1960. The first one concert took place on January 2nd, 1961. In April, she went on tour with Dumont, who sang *Les Amants* in a duet with her. She is hospitalized again in May. The press discusses the possibility of cancer. The death of Marguerite Monnot, on October 12th, is a great shock for Édith.
- **1962:** Édith Piaf lives in Paris, at Boulevard Lannes. She has a small courtyard where she sometimes arranges for her exclusive service: songwriters Charles Dumont, Francis Lai, Michel Vaucaire and Pierre Delanoë, journalist and singer Claude Figus, and, especially, a young hairdresser of Greek origin: Théophranis Lamboukas, whom she renames Théo Sarapo before marrying him on October 9th. She will sing *À quoi ça sert l'amour* with him, and will perform it at the Eiffel Tower. Increasingly weakened by her excessive drug use, she is no longer capable of performing certain pieces, like *Hymne à l'amour*, but this does not prevent her from going on tour at the end of the year.
- **1963:** In February, Édith Piaf performs at the Théâtre Bobino. She will give her last concerts on March 30th and 31st. In April, she sinks into a hepatic coma for 4 days, then leaves to rest on the Côte-d'Azur. She will be hospitalized several times in Cannes, until October 10th, when she dies during her sleep. Théo Sarapo–faithful to her last wishes, which were to be buried in Paris after death–brings her body back to the capital, where the death is officially announced on October 11th. Édith Piaf rests in the cemetery of Père-Lachaise, with her father Louis Gassion and her daughter Marcelle.

About the Author

Born in Remiremont (France) in 1960, Thierry Rollet has devoted himself to literature since the age of 15. Associate to Gens de Lettres de France. He published his first book at age 21 and is now at his 38th published book. First a teacher, he founded in 1999 the Scribo company, which handles the distribution of books, literary advice to authors wanting to be published, training in French / English and a writing workshop. Thierry Rollet has published novels, collections of short stories, historical accounts, and many novels in magazines and on the Internet.

You can connect with me on:
- http://ecrivainthierryrollet.e-monsite.com
- http://www.facebook.com/thierryrolletecrivain

www.ingramcontent.com/pod-product-compliance
Lightning Source LLC
LaVergne TN
LVHW051710080426
835511LV00017B/2841